The Radiance Of The Little Girl:

Embracing Self-Worth

By Aaron Fields

Illustrated by Umar Altaf

The happiness, beauty and good health that you see in a little girl's face is a blessing.

Aaron Fields

In a world that often fails to see,

The worth and beauty of the little girl's glee.

It's vital for her to know and embrace,

The power and worth within her grace.

With every breath she takes, she will rise,

Embracing her roots, reaching for the skies.

For her value is not defined by others' gaze,

But by the love and confidence she displays.

In a society that may try to dim her light,

She will shine bright, with all her might.

For she is a symbol of resilience and grace,

A reflection of beauty in every space.

So let the little girl value herself,

For in her heart lies endless wealth

A treasure trove of wisdom and power,

A reminder that she is a blooming flower.

May she always remember that without a doubt,

That her worth is boundless, inside and out.

For the little girl's value is a precious treasure,

A testament to her beauty and pleasure.

END

www.ingramcontent.com/pod-product-compliance
Lightning Source LLC
Chambersburg PA
CBHW040035110426
42741CB00030B/27

9 781953 962478